# on the way to Amen

## Lily Mars

*on the way to Amen*
ISBN 978-0-578-57646-6
LilyMars Press
copyright LilyMars 2019

Other books by LilyMars
**heart s t u c k open**

Printed in the United States of America
Available on Amazon

Designed and produced by Heidi Connolly
Harvard Girl Word Services www.HarvardGirlEdits.com

Cover photo by Charles David Harless, Jr.
Author photo by Destiny Spanier

LilyMars Press

# Dedication

for Nelson
who is big on Dreams

# Acknowledgments

My everlasting gratitude goes to the Bandon Writers Group for their weekly support, and particularly to the indomitable Peggy Gardner, without whose unflagging editorial collaboration this book would never have been born.

*Be like the bird, who*
*Pausing in her flight awhile*
*On limb too slight*
*Feels it give way beneath her,*
*Yet sings*
*Knowing she hath wings*

–Victor Hugo (translated from the French)

# Contents

# interval

while there is

a whole life

in between


it is birth

and death

that wake us up


the rest

is barely

seen

## blues

the bluejays have
gone missing
from the scene
outside our window
those squawky dependable
rabble rousers

we had forgotten about
their beauty
when they took away
their blue

# muse

precisely when
you begin
to believe
she is gone
for good
when you
willfully turn
your back

she is here again
most likely when
you are driving
in your car
or when you
are kneeling
in the garden
with your fingers
caked in mud

she will be whispering
in that maddening
barely audible
way she has
of urging you on
enticing you out
of your sinful faithless
pout

if she arrives
at three in the morning
she will shout you
out of bed

be advised to pay attention
she is only saying
it this way
once

# middles

I will not ask
you to tell
me the story
of your life
you cannot tell it
you do not know the beginning
you cannot know the end

some parts in between
are a bit of a muddle
some things
you have completely forgotten
misremembered or
have somehow become
altered along the way

just ask a few
characters who show up
in your story
ask them who you have been
in theirs
tell them who they are
in yours

there is life
and there is story
do not fall in love with the story
you are concocting
as you go
along

## write away

for the mouse
there shall be
a new story
that will exclude
hunger
and fear

a conclusion
with a happy ending
invented to release
me

# I Went Out

into the world for something else
 chili powder
 whipping cream
 sunflower bouquets

and picked up an idea
 maybe just a notion
 a terwilliger
 a prickle

brought it home still warm
 a loaf
 a seedling
 a wrinkled thrift store blouse

let it rise
tucked it in
pressed it

if it were a kitten
held it
fed it
let it explore

if it were a plant
placed it in the sun
overwatered it
revived it
wrote about it

but the notion
the idea
gets carried everywhere
grows cold and empty
in a folder on a desk
ends up hidden in some
forgotten drawer

now look
here it is

# Acting

There is a story
to this coat
and a story
to these boots
Everything has its story
Someday you will
become one too

Now tell me the story
of your morning
injected with last
night's dreaming
During your day
as you step and you speak
you may be
an actor in an unproduced drama

No wonder
the search for identity reigns
when scene is detached
from scenario
You are living
the evolving epiphanies
of your ancestors'
unknowing

You receive
a signal
from time
to time

# in time

we spend our days
insulated between
earth and sky
dependent upon
floor and ceiling
determined to believe
we act alone

      maybe we just float
      in the stream
      with the cool cool current
      that rushes through this hot moment
                  in time

# tides

I once knew
a boy
who gave me
his first
gaze

I once knew
a boy
who began
my lessons
in everything
my schooling
missed

I once knew
a boy
who goes on
invisibly

like the waves
he recedes
then flows forth
enchanting the shores
with possibilities

## seduction

listening to Leonard
everybody knows
Suzanne takes you down
hallelujah
lyrics so poisonously
beautiful
makes me wonder
exactly when
I swallowed
the enchanting
black pill
of sorrow

maybe it happened
in church
where a child might
easily drown in
her sea of sins
as mysterious Latin hymns
soared in majesty
mourning a bloody death

maybe the unquenchable
serial loneliness
of a bookish girl with
too many siblings
and too many jolting
dislocations to
unfamiliar places

maybe my soul
was a waiting pool
for the raging storm of 60's angst
and then Leonard
came along
and sang

## dust to dustbunnies

for the closeted
confessing of imaginary sins
in the dark

for the Sunday
swallowing of Body
and Blood

for the eery lintballs
drifting underneath
her childhood bed

mortality monsters
stuck inside
her head

she was much too
young to apprehend
the world
is not without
end

Amen.

## wings upon the window

the mistake

of the dove

resembles

the outline

of an angel

on this early

sunstruck morning


you can see

the perfect head

the tail feathers

the open wings


corollary

to a footnote

to a myth

## quills

'twas not the postage
got us airborne
our ink
on paper
signified

all the wistful people
without wings
we used
our words
to fly

## once more with wings

next time I think
I might
come back avian
not night hawk nor dove
nor talony falcon
something dark
and wild and plain
destined to live an uncaged life
brief and simple
a builder of nests
confident of my mission

next time I hope
for installed memory
to distinguish glass panes
from open windows
a black bird perhaps
the better to hide
through the predatory nights
and sing songs to describe
the terrible beauty of my existence
and use my wings to beat
upon heaven's door

next time I believe
could be the last time
I plan ahead
and arrive readymade
with strange skin
and unfamiliar bones
maybe even feathers
to test the wind
to learn my way home
and forget all over again

# circulation

your bookshelves
a museum
to the thoughts
of others

your writing
a unique
testimony
to your life

you know
time travel
is not
science fiction

witness these
brittle love letters
burnished
and forgotten

the yearning
bright and raw
as a ritual
bloodletting

## apertures

the room
where I sleep
has windows and mirrors
closets and doors

bookshelves
skylights
paintings
walls

sanctuary and storehouse
a place for
surrender and renewal
awakening and dreams

looking out
looking in
seeing my way
through

at night
between covers
chapter breaks
offer openings

## thorns

my friend wrote to thank me
for the roses
she said she couldn't think
why she hadn't planted roses

so I wrote back about the roses
about how they are called Chrysler Imperial
and how every deep red petal smells like rose heaven
and how my maternal grandfather
who was vice president of Chrysler
had a poodle named Impy
and how when I was a child that dog fed my starved dreams
and how Papa showed me his cherry trees
and his red red roses
and how this deep velvet scent carries through
to this day
decades later
thousands of miles
millions of roses
from MIchigan

## touch

on this ordinary
night secure in
the other one
breathing

now hearing
only silence

here is my hand
on your stomach
here is my hand
on your heart

you stir in
sleep wondering
is this touch
desire

# hello again

all
relationships
are fragile

click
click
click

we are not good
about
goodbye

we are engineered
to keep
going

step
after
step

since we learned
to walk
we have been told
don't
fall
down

but then
we do

## Stillness Exaggerated

If you pay attention

to the summer swallows

who build their mud nests

on the wall outside your window

you witness

the mindless task

of survival

You begin

to understand the way

that frantic nurturing

must succumb

to relentless leaving

## angles

walk yourself around and round
look from sky
look from ground
crawl yourself right under
ignore lightning
attend thunder
each view offers its own wonder
that's how the pruning gets done

say your subject
is an elegant Japanese
maple left to grow wild
year after year
the thought of one cut brings fear
one day you know
that the time has come
to begin the walkaround

perhaps there's a poem
you've been meaning to write
a vase of flowers to arrange
a constellation to discover in the night
when you get up close things look strange
move on back maybe ten steps away
then perhaps what looked like disarray
presents itself like sky

# Back to Quiet

The solar lights
on the back deck
are still going strong
at 1:23 when the cats
start tussling
and wake me up

I had never noticed before
the way the miniature lighthouse
casts its long rays
in a perfect circle
across the night floor

One cat and I sit
at the window
and stare at that
awhile

Only our breath
hangs in the still air
and anything
feels possible

# where silence reigns

hushed places

libraries

churches

forests after snows


waiting spaces

where God whispers

but never speaks

one word

# infinities

some things are too big

to be seen

galaxies

night monsters

godspace


some things are too small

to be recognized

the oak sprout

a hummingbird egg

an ordinary kindness


like the infinitesimal

pale green spider

that arrived this morning

on my garden basil

some things

are too tiny

to save

## cyclone

chop up the night
into bite-size pieces
no need to swallow
every dream whole

though I can't tell
what it's doing
something is surely
in the chewing

hopes and fears
decades away
mixing up
whirling around
until every
thing
goes
down

## connect

untouched
he becomes
untouchable

unheard
      inaudible
unseen
      invisible
unmoved
      immobile
unknown
      unknowable

he turns off
the switches
one
by
one

## Sharp Things

the cat has been busy in the night
tearing open the bread bag
with her teeth
nature provides her with every
implement useful
for her survival

we are bony soft humans
who manicure and pedicure
more and more we leave the chopping
to someone else

Manson and his girls woke me up long ago
there would never again
be a knife on my
kitchen counter

and yet

we hone our sharp minds
our sharper tongues

in the end we hope to slit
the bewitching throat
of our assassin

## driving home

this pink mountain
lasts less
than one minute
it is
the shortest day

a compensatory
moon hangs
for an instant
suspended
from a silver
jet stream
two ornaments
in the swiftly
morphing sky
an hour later
black velvet
reigns
the first star
a jeweled tear

## some boundaries

I live

beneath the marbled masterpiece
of a somewhat scurrilous sky

inside the cracked glass globe
of a sometimes lighted lamp

outside the community concert
of teeming forested voices


i live

amidst the swirl of swallows
and their petulant progeny

atop tortuous tunnels
of the blinded

beside the beleaguered
and the brave


between the root
the blossom
and the fruit

I live

## Gift

What will you give
your son
on his birth day
this year?

How about
a photograph
of his handsome
summer face

    on that sun-drowned late August afternoon when
    he went camping with some friends and thank
    God one of them captured this perfect image

The man at
the cemetery
assures me
the smile
in this gravestone cameo
will last
for ever.

# here again

here in late summer
strong heat hazy
all things pale blue and bone
seared beyond recognition

scrubby low hills
barely scratch the leaden sky
overseeing useless bleached
pastures

parched landscape sparks
fever burn of memories
that threaten to emerge
like crop marks during drought

just beneath the surface
of any sunny August day
a small blue car
falls off the edge

> over and
> over and
> over
> again

**sufferance**

we dance
around this
all our lives

sometimes eyes open
sometimes blindfolded
so often astonished
by the beauty
by the savagery

all by itself
the pain will not
kill you

the anesthetic
will

## low tide

everything
at the beach
is both
old
and
new

change starts out slow
ends up fast
because
there is
a finish

if you walk

out far

enough

on the newly naked sand

you can view
the undrowned
starfish
gracefully lifting
a finger to
the moon

## dark fruit

slice out
the middle
of the night
now

this is
the worm hole
in the apple
or
the seeds
in the apple
core

the message
in the bottle
headed off
to shore

the hidden heart
of the armored
artichoke

and something
more

# If True

if true
the hyenas
escaped the zoo
we may be terrified
or laughing

if true
we knew
grasshoppers were blue
the fields would require
a whole new palette

if true
the planet
is at our mercy
what is the point
of planting this tree

if it is true
there is no God
then we may be laughing
or terrified

## the widows

one is grieving
one is leaving
one is working through

one goes forward
one looks back
one designs her next tattoo

imagine the too-quiet room
and rooms
and rooms
and rooms

if it happens to me
and I live separately
this yawning space will expand
and invite
another song

## How Are You

new widow
inferno refugee

shut in
shut out

hero
saint

shorn and unshorn
born and unborn

survivors
to be kind

will tell you

I am fine

# repairs

how to
put together
the pieces

to fashion
something
whole

a job
best done
inside
out

the mending
of tattered
edges
hardly leaves
a mark

perhaps God
is a seamstress

sewing up
the seems

# epiphany

five days
after Christmas
she came downstairs
to find the fire had gone out
her husband slouched
on the sofa
as if dreaming

in his hands a list
of mundane errands
the next steps
to prepare
for his perfect projects

she told us
he always said
in the end
he would have to be
carried out
feet first

some furniture
had to be rearranged
so his body
could be turned
around

to make things right
on his last
trip out
the door


in fond remembrance of Dave Cornell

# ambush

my mother

her mother

and her mother's mom

each outlived

her desire

to go on

and faded away

in a room far astray

from family

down the line

here am I

on the road

endlessly waiting

my empty suitcase

full of questions

## open book

we are going much too fast
to stop on the highway
when I see a red hardcover
on the side of the road
pages beckoning
in the breeze

my partner who is at the wheel
insists that turning around
would be folly
and so we go on by

perhaps we passed up a classic
maybe a signed Keats
or possibly Dosteovsky
or better yet
someone's thoughtful diary
but we
shall never know

## conundrums

I make piles
and unpile them

I fill files
and unfile them

I sleep soundly
yet sound sleepy

I scream screams
then unscream them

I dream dreams
then undream them

      unsing the songs that I have sung

      unhang the laundry I have hung

      unvow the promises I have made

I am soaked
from unweeping

## Today

someone is getting married today

someone is going home

in the morning a young father is swept out to sea
his baby boy strapped to his back
         one tiny shoe will come ashore tomorrow
          that's all

my son calls me in the afternoon to talk about
the car crash just down the road
where he had just been nonchalantly
discussing brake linings
with a neighbor when
the jarring thud
burrows into his brain

the unthinking rush to the site
witness to the dazed driver
        quite suddenly a survivor
        now the owner of a brand new life
        shouting into compacted space
        holding his head in his hands

witness to the breathless bodies
only moments ago whole and laughing
determined to rev up
for one more race

someone is being born today

someone is writing a poem

## two miles

those two miles
were always there
just waiting to be walked

those two hands
were always there
just waiting to be clapped

your loved one
daily in the chair
just waiting to be missed

seven books upon the table
waiting to be opened
three words all lined up
waiting to be said

two unspeaking people
as the day comes to its end
there will be no waiting
in the country of the dead

## levels

does cloud descend
to become fog
or
does fog rise up
to become cloud

there is science
to explore the mechanics
of things    but
science can never
interpret what the eye sees
explain what the heart knows

you can run out of air
within atmosphere

## Flowers Home

Norma was a city girl
and a lefty
Arthur a right-handed
farm boy

they found they agreed
on the shape of the world
and its relationship
to the heavens above
so they followed each other
from one surprising place to another
and ended up owning
some secluded coastal acres
then set about making
the land their home

one day Norma and Arthur
and his right-handed sister
were clearing a trail through the forest
when they looked up from their task
to discover that the sun had disappeared
behind the tall trees
and they had lost their compass

left-handed Norma
told her companions
they were going in circles
because all day
she had been looking down
noting the yellow violas silently
marking every turn
so they followed
the flowers home

# freight

the haunting sound
of trains in the night
calls out the old ghosts
recalibrates the rhythm
of my wary heart

this town belongs
to trains in the night
racketing along their
endless tracks
blasting me open

get out of the way say
the trains in the night
they always seem to be
circling around then
rushing off again

## planet without tears

the child perches atop
her backyard swingset
singing to the lonely moon

she has just been told
her family is moving again


fifty years later she
listens as her daughter's daughter
dances to that wolf song

throws back her shiny head
lets go her joyous howl

        we sit here
        in the present
        where the past
        becomes the future
        and the future is
        on its way

# earthworm half life

one can never tell
what one will see
whilst minding one's
own business

a fish in a tree
a mermaid at sea
and then one day
oh glory be
a hungry newt
biting off his supper

then the diner goes
one way
the dinner
another

## flash

from up close
a nuclear blast
will melt you
straight back to the molten core

miles away from
the explosion
the sighted are blinded
the blind girl sees
a flash of light

in one of those grainy
old war documentaries
you can listen to a survivor
almost affectionately
recall

how she used
the ashes
from her poetry books
for tooth powder

## Survival

we are born deceived
and practice deception
all our lives

how nearly instinctual
the turn away
the shifting gaze
practicing, practicing

think Adam
think Eve
so briefly
innocent

every moment
something hidden
every calculated move
aimed at
the impossible

## at the dollar store

I came in to look
for stickers
for the grandkids
who like such things

some photo frames
three blue plates
and some mothballs

some generic shampoo
some pencils
and some bows

at the checkout
just south of the lip balm
and the chewing gum
I saw rosaries

hanging on a single hook
in pink
and in black
and in blue

I could not choose
a color

## just asking

she refuses a bandaid
when she scrapes her knee
because it will hurt to take off

> Mom told me not to fall
> and then I fell

she reminds me of things
that I once knew

> Is this book
> fiction or nonfiction
> or maybe it's realistic
> fiction

she erupts with inconvenient questions

> How many children do you have
> What happened to your brown hair
> Who is Jesus

when I hesitate
she hurries off

> don't fall down
> I am thinking
> while I stand still
> figuring out
> my answer

## sailing

sailboat lessons taught
my minister friend
lifesaving skills
about how a swimmer
in distress
might sink both
victim #1 and
victim #2

we were all set
he would later write
to move on
in life secure
in the confidence
we could
rescue
anyone

## 21st Century Kids

their childhood goes by
at the speed of light
what they know about fast
is their barefoot flight
our imagination may
not be equal to
the world that awaits
so we step up
the pace
of our beach walk

## pithing poem

the new kids are strange
they have other dreams
you can play cards with cards
if you shut off the screen

but after a round or two
of old maid or fish
the five-year-old tells you
his fondest wish

mama, get a robot
that looks just like me
and then you can play
whenever you please

the pot is slowly heating up
the frogs have been dissected
the brain may have been rendered moot
but the heart goes on and on

# aquarium

all beauty
no brain
no spine
no heart
no will

the jellyfish

float

you can't
look away
from their
nonchalant
exposures

# memoir

she always said
she would never
return
she insisted
she would not
because she
could not


although one day
she went home
she would
always say
she did not
because she
had not

## Poseidon

then came the morning
when our surviving
children stood
with me at your bedside
their seasick eyes
seeking out
the bright line measuring
the ending
of their father's life
on the beeping screen
  it took so long

when it was over
we walked away
drenched and scorched
blinded and numb
fleeing our personal apocalypse
not unlike the stricken audience
of some B movie thriller
where a few unlucky
shipwreck survivors
go straight home
  to bed

# measurements

she collects cookbooks

she collects frames

she does not use them but stashes them in closets

dutiful daughter she

keeps her parents' ashes

in the cuddleroom separately and she checks there frequently

in case they have puffed out

every september she

makes sure to send

flowers down the creek near the place where she grew up

and 2 Tablespoons go in

after that whether they

mingle or not

is beyond her control

# changes

they come in
on winter wood
they ride in
within crimson
rose petals

and just like that
their world transforms

they have no expectation
of permanence
their gauzy webs
are made for
reweaving

they have no notion
of their breathing
nor do they
lament their labor

as they make

new camps

in the corners

of my corners

## Mia Beloved

outside soft rain
caresses the pines
I slide open the window
turn a page in my notebook
three lines greet me
their existence unremembered
devised in a different world

Mia. Beloved
Zoe. Life
Avalon. Island of apples

clothed in wishes
she passes through
my waking dreams
and is gone

## a choreography

witness the daughter
caught hard
by the dream

now that my
grown child
is careening
through the dream

watch her dance
watch her swirl
watch her perform
the endless tasks
she won't recall
once the dream
is done

in a moment
the years
go spinning back

I am she
she is me

both mother and babe
dervishing away

## swimming under the stars

you are not the morning

you are not the night

you are not the darkness

you are not the light


you are not a dream

you are not a sign

you were not my destiny

you were not mine

# This Is a Test

Her predicament
is reminiscent
of the plight
of the Dragonistas
when intractable
Plutonic sympathies
unmitigated by the efforts
of Clovis and Byrnes
on the unforgettable
afternoon when
sharp fallout from
the eternal equinox
lopped off
some citizen's head
and led to the
Peppercornian Wars

Unimpressed by
the prospect of rising seas
she dreams of yoking
the poles
of heaven and earth
to the belly
of the first winter calf
and then heaving
the whole shebang
over the ledge
of Prelantis

Perhaps she hopes for salvation
but everyone knows
it is our destiny
to be crushed
on the Rocks
of Ages
and silted
into the Sands
of Time

## capture

we hang chimes
so we might hear
the wind
glass baubles
to reflect the sun
solar gadgets
to catch the light
in preparation
for dark of night
we direct heat
and cold
like little gods

plant for food
and decoration
chant and sing
for meditation
shelve forests of books
for rumination
all attempts
at illuminating
the least of
our knowing

## World Not New, Unbrave

I will be sharing
my bean burrito
with the cat
when I hear the news.

After 146 years
the circus
is folding
along with so many other
simple pleasures
of childhood.

> someone home to answer the door
> everywhere you could walk your world
> open fields and woods to explore
> the wonder of elephants without the

angst

It feels like
a kind of eclipse
a darkening of the known sun
the closing lid of future.

## salvation

sounds soothing
a balm
something lovingly applied
by a caring hand
to your wounds

sounds seekable
a hug
something of value
a treasure
at rainbow's end

sounds authentic
a goal
something benevolent
a summation
of good turns

salvation is
a word only letters
apart from
      salivate
      salvage
      savage

salvation sounds
like rescue
but from what
you cannot say

you must find meaning
wherever you may

## this life and after

Time has taken
care of what might
have been

Time is a silken
silver strand
picked out by the sun

carry them with you
carry you with them

Time is forever
on its way to
gild another Spring

carry you with them
carry them with you

## constellations

cinder cone and continent
crater and crevasse

river, bayou, sea
canyon, dune, lagoon
archipelago

exist inside
amoebae
and bus-size whales


each of us
carries whole
worlds within worlds
while we remain
stuck to this planet

still

looking up
to the stars

## walking around in the mystery

galaxies outside
universes within
we spend our lives
balanced between
terrifying worlds
of wonder
granted more questions
than answers

is there
another way
you would want it
to be

www.ingramcontent.com/pod-product-compliance
Lightning Source LLC
Chambersburg PA
CBHW022008090426
42741CB00007B/944